# Café de Paris

## Authentic Recipes from the Heart of France

## Lui Giuseppe

# Café de Paris

## © Copyright 2024 By Lui Giuseppe

## All Rights Reserved

either directly or indirectly. Respective authors own all copyrights not held by the publisher. The information herein is offered for informational purposes solely, and is universal as so.

The presentation of the information is without contract or any type of guarantee assurance. The trademarks that are used are without any consent, and the publication of the trademark is without permission or backing by the trademark owner. All trademarks and brands within this book are for clarifying purposes only and are owned by the owners themselves, not affiliated with this document.

# TABLE OF CONTENTS

# Introduction

## Welcome to Café de Paris

Welcome to "Café de Paris: Authentic Recipes from the Heart of France." This book is a journey through the culinary delights of French cuisine, bringing the flavors and traditions of Parisian cafés into your kitchen. Whether you're a seasoned cook or a beginner, this collection of recipes and tips will help you create delicious, authentic French dishes with confidence and joy.

## The Essence of French Cooking

French cooking is renowned for its elegance, simplicity, and focus on high-quality ingredients. At its heart, French cuisine is about celebrating the natural flavors of fresh, seasonal produce. Techniques such as sautéing, braising, and roasting are used to enhance, rather than mask, these flavors. French meals are often enjoyed leisurely, with an emphasis on savoring each bite and enjoying the company of friends and family.

# Ingredients and Tools

To create authentic French dishes, it's important to start with the right ingredients and tools. Here are some essentials you'll need:

**Butter:** French butter is often richer and creamier due to its higher fat content.

**Cream:** Use heavy cream for sauces and desserts.

**Cheeses:** From Brie to Roquefort, French cheeses are integral to many recipes.

Herbs: Fresh herbs like thyme, rosemary, and tarragon add depth to dishes.

**wine:** Both red and white wines are used in cooking to add flavor and complexity.

Baking tools: A good rolling pin, pastry brush, and baking sheets are essential for pastries and breads.

# Tips for Success in French Cooking

Read Recipes Thoroughly: Before you start cooking, read the recipe from beginning to end.

Prep Ingredients: Have all your ingredients measured and prepared before you start cooking.

Quality Matters: Use the best quality ingredients you can find.

**Take Your Time:** French cooking often involves multiple steps. Don't rush the process.

Taste as You Go: Adjust seasonings to your preference.

## How to Use This Book

This book is organized into chapters that cover various aspects of French cuisine, from breakfast pastries to main courses and desserts. Each chapter includes a selection of recipes, along with tips and techniques to help you master each dish. Feel free to jump around and explore the recipes that appeal to you the most. Enjoy the journey through the flavors and traditions of French cooking!

# Chapter 1: The Parisian Breakfast

## 1.1 Classic Croissants

*ingredients:*

- 500g all-purpose flour
- 10g salt
- 80g sugar
- 30g unsalted butter, softened
- 10g instant yeast
- 300ml cold milk
- 250g unsalted butter, chilled

**Instructions:**

Prepare the Dough: In a large bowl, combine the flour, salt, sugar, and yeast. Add the softened butter and milk, and mix until a dough forms. Knead for about 10 minutes until smooth. Cover and refrigerate for at least 2 hours.

Prepare the Butter Block: Place the chilled butter between two sheets of parchment paper. Using a rolling pin, pound the butter into a flat, even rectangle about 1/2 inch thick. Refrigerate until firm.

Roll Out the Dough: On a lightly floured surface, roll the dough into a large rectangle. Place the butter block in the center and fold the dough over the butter, sealing the edges.

Laminate the Dough: Roll out the dough into a long rectangle, then fold it into thirds, like a letter. Turn the dough 90 degrees and repeat the rolling and folding process two more times. Refrigerate for 30 minutes between each fold.

Shape the Croissants: Roll the dough into a large rectangle and cut it into triangles. Roll each triangle from the base to the tip to form a crescent shape. Place on a baking sheet and let rise for about 1 hour.

Bake: Preheat the oven to 200°C (400°F). Brush the croissants with an egg wash and bake for 15-20 minutes until golden brown and flaky. Enjoy warm!

## 1.2 Pain au Chocolat

*ingredients:*

- 500g all-purpose flour

- 10g salt
- 80g sugar
- 30g unsalted butter, softened
- 10g instant yeast
- 300ml cold milk
- 250g unsalted butter, chilled
- 200g dark chocolate, cut into sticks

**Instructions:**

Prepare the Dough: In a large bowl, combine the flour, salt, sugar, and yeast. Add the softened butter and milk, and mix until a dough forms. Knead for about 10 minutes until smooth. Cover and refrigerate for at least 2 hours.

Prepare the Butter Block: Place the chilled butter between two sheets of parchment paper. Using a rolling pin, pound the butter into a flat, even rectangle about 1/2 inch thick. Refrigerate until firm.

Laminate the Dough: On a lightly floured surface, roll the dough into a large rectangle. Place the butter block in the center and fold the dough over the butter, sealing the edges. Roll out the dough into a long rectangle, then fold it into thirds, like a letter. Turn the dough 90 degrees and repeat the rolling and folding process two more times. Refrigerate for 30 minutes between each fold.

Shape the Pain au Chocolat: Roll the dough into a large rectangle and cut it into smaller rectangles. Place a stick of chocolate at one end of each rectangle, then roll the dough around the chocolate. Place on a baking sheet and let rise for about 1 hour.

Bake: Preheat the oven to 200°C (400°F). Brush the pain au chocolat with an egg wash and bake for 15-20 minutes until golden brown and flaky. Enjoy warm!

## 1.3 Baguettes and Tartines

*Ingredients for Baguettes:*

- 500g all-purpose flour
- 10g salt
- 10g instant yeast
- 300ml warm water

**Instructions:**

Prepare the Dough: In a large bowl, combine the flour, salt, and yeast. Add the warm water and mix until a dough forms. Knead for about 10 minutes until smooth and elastic. Cover and let rise for 1 hour or until doubled in size.

Shape the Baguettes: Divide the dough into three equal pieces. Roll each piece into a long cylinder and place on a baking sheet. Cover and let rise for 30 minutes.

Bake: Preheat the oven to 220°C (430°F). Make a few diagonal slashes on the top of each baguette with a sharp knife. Bake for 20-25 minutes until golden brown and crisp. Let cool before slicing.

**Ingredients for Tartines:**

- Freshly baked baguettes
- Butter, softened
- Assorted toppings (e.g., jam, cheese, ham, avocado, smoked salmon)

**Instructions:**

Prepare the Tartines: Slice the baguette into pieces. Spread each slice with butter and add your choice of toppings.

Serve: *Serve the tartines immediately, either as part of a breakfast spread or as a light meal.*

# 1.4 French Omelettes

*ingredients*:

- ★ 4 large eggs
- ★ Salt and pepper to taste
- ★ 2 tablespoons unsalted butter
- ★ Fresh herbs (optional, e.g., chives, parsley)

**Instructions**:

Prepare the Eggs: In a bowl, whisk the eggs with salt and pepper until well combined.

Cook the Omelette: In a non-stick skillet, melt the butter over medium heat. Pour in the eggs and let them cook undisturbed for a few seconds until they start to set. Using a spatula, gently stir the eggs, pushing them towards the center until they are mostly set but still slightly runny on top.

Finish and Serve: Fold the omelette in half and slide it onto a plate. Sprinkle with fresh herbs if desired. Serve immediately.

Café au Lait and Other Morning Beverages

# 1.5 Café au Lait

**ingredients**:

- 1 cup strong brewed coffee
- 1 cup steamed milk

*Instructions:*

Brew the Coffee: Brew a strong cup of coffee using your preferred method.

Steam the Milk: Heat milk in a saucepan over medium heat until steaming, or use a milk frother.

Combine and Serve: Pour the coffee into a large mug and add the steamed milk. Serve immediately.

## Other Morning Beverages

Hot Chocolate: Melt 50g of dark chocolate with 1 cup of milk in a saucepan over medium heat. Stir until smooth and serve hot.

Fresh Orange Juice: Squeeze the juice from 4-5 fresh oranges. Serve immediately for the best flavor.

tea: Brew your favorite tea and serve with a slice of lemon or a splash of milk.

# Chapter 2: Boulangerie and Patisserie

## 2.1 The Art of Baking Bread

*Ingredients:*

- 500g all-purpose flour
- 10g salt
- 10g instant yeast
- 300ml warm water

*Instructions:*

Prepare the Dough: In a large bowl, combine the flour, salt, and yeast. Add the warm water and mix until a dough forms. Knead for about 10 minutes until smooth and elastic. Cover and let rise for 1 hour or until doubled in size.

Shape the Bread: Punch down the dough and shape it into a loaf or desired shape. Place on a baking sheet or in a loaf pan. Cover and let rise for another 30 minutes.

Bake: Preheat the oven to 220°C (430°F). Make a few slashes on the top of the loaf with a sharp knife. Bake for 30-35 minutes until golden brown and hollow sounding when tapped on the bottom. Let cool before slicing.

## 2.2 Elegant Pastries

***Ingredients for Puff Pastry:***

- 250g all-purpose flour
- 1/2 teaspoon salt
- 250g unsalted butter, chilled and cut into small pieces
- 120ml cold water

***Instructions:***

Prepare the Dough: In a bowl, mix the flour and salt. Add the chilled butter and mix until it resembles coarse crumbs. Slowly add the cold water and mix until the dough comes together. Shape into a rectangle, wrap in plastic wrap, and refrigerate for at least 1 hour.

Laminate the Dough: Roll the dough into a large rectangle on a lightly floured surface. Fold the dough into thirds, like a letter. Turn the dough 90 degrees and repeat the rolling and folding process three more times. Refrigerate for 30 minutes between each fold.

Shape and Bake: Roll out the laminated dough to your desired thickness and cut into shapes for your pastry. Place on a baking sheet and bake at 200°C (400°F) for 15-20 minutes until golden brown and puffed. Fill or top with desired fillings or glazes.

## 2.3 Quiches and Savory Tarts

***Ingredients for Quiche Lorraine:***

- 1 pie crust (store-bought or homemade)
- 200g bacon, diced
- 1 small onion, finely chopped
- 3 large eggs
- 200ml heavy cream
- Salt and pepper to taste
- 100g Gruyère cheese, grated

***Instructions***:

Prepare the Crust: Preheat the oven to 180°C (350°F). Roll out the pie crust and fit it into a tart pan. Prick the bottom with a fork and pre-bake for 10 minutes.

Prepare the Filling: In a skillet, cook the bacon until crispy. Remove and drain on paper towels. In the same skillet, cook the onion until soft. In a bowl, whisk together the eggs, cream, salt, and pepper.

Assemble and Bake: Spread the bacon and onion over the pre-baked crust. Pour the egg mixture over the top and sprinkle with grated cheese. Bake for 25-30 minutes until the filling is set and the top is golden brown. Let cool slightly before slicing.

## 2.4 Madeleines and Financiers

***Ingredients for Madeleines:***

- 130g all-purpose flour
- 1/2 teaspoon baking powder
- 2 large eggs
- 130g sugar
- 1 teaspoon vanilla extract
- 100g unsalted butter, melted
- Zest of 1 lemon

***Instructions:***

Prepare the Batter: In a bowl, whisk together the flour and baking powder. In another bowl, beat the eggs and sugar until pale and thick. Add the vanilla extract and lemon zest. Fold in the flour mixture and then the melted butter. Cover and refrigerate for at least 1 hour.

Bake: Preheat the oven to 190°C (375°F). Butter and flour a madeleine pan. Spoon the batter into the molds, filling each about three-quarters full. Bake for 10-12 minutes until the edges are golden brown and the centers are set. Remove from the pan and cool on a wire rack.

## 2.5 Ingredients for Financiers:

- 100g almond flour
- 50g all-purpose flour
- 150g powdered sugar
- 1/4 teaspoon salt
- 4 large egg whites
- 100g unsalted butter, melted and browned
- 1 teaspoon vanilla extract

*Instructions*:

Prepare the Batter: In a bowl, whisk together the almond flour, all-purpose flour, powdered sugar, and salt. In another bowl, whisk the egg whites until frothy. Add the egg whites to the dry ingredients and mix until combined. Stir in the browned butter and vanilla extract.

Bake: Preheat the oven to 180°C (350°F). Butter and flour a financier mold or mini muffin tin. Spoon the batter into the molds, filling each about two-thirds full. Bake for 15-18 minutes until golden brown and a toothpick inserted into the center comes out clean. Remove from the pan and cool on a wire rack.

## 2.6 Eclairs and Choux Pastry

*Ingredients for Choux Pastry:*

- 120ml water
- 120ml milk
- 100g unsalted butter
- 1/2 teaspoon salt
- 1 tablespoon sugar
- 130g all-purpose flour
- 4 large eggs

**Instructions:**

Prepare the Dough: In a saucepan, combine the water, milk, butter, salt, and sugar. Bring to a boil over medium heat. Add the flour all at once and stir vigorously until the mixture forms a ball and pulls away from the sides of the pan. Remove from heat and let cool slightly.

Add the Eggs: Transfer the dough to a bowl. Add the eggs one at a time, beating well after each addition, until the dough is smooth and glossy.

Shape and Bake: Preheat the oven to 200°C (400°F). Pipe the dough onto a baking sheet lined with parchment paper, forming long strips for eclairs or small mounds for cream puffs. Bake for 20-25 minutes until golden brown and puffed. Let cool completely.

## 2.7 Ingredients for Eclair Filling and Glaze:

- 200ml heavy cream
- 2 tablespoons powdered sugar
- 1 teaspoon vanilla extract
- 150g dark chocolate, melted

*Instructions*:

Prepare the Filling: In a bowl, whip the heavy cream with the powdered sugar and vanilla extract until stiff peaks form. Transfer to a piping bag.

Fill the Eclairs: Once the choux pastry is cool, slice the eclairs in half lengthwise. Pipe the whipped cream into the bottom half of each eclair and place the top half back on.

Glaze the Eclairs: Dip the top of each eclair in the melted chocolate and let set. Serve immediately.

# Chapter 3: Starters and Small Plates

## 3.1 Classic French Onion Soup

**ingredients:**

- 3 large onions, thinly sliced
- 4 tablespoons unsalted butter
- 1 tablespoon olive oil
- 1 teaspoon sugar
- 3 cloves garlic, minced
- 1/2 cup dry white wine
- 1.5 liters beef broth
- 1 bay leaf
- 1 teaspoon fresh thyme leaves (or 1/2 teaspoon dried thyme)
- Salt and pepper to taste
- 1 baguette, sliced
- 2 cups grated Gruyère cheese

*Instructions:*

Caramelize the Onions: In a large pot, melt the butter with the olive oil over medium heat. Add the onions and cook, stirring occasionally, until they are soft and caramelized, about 25-30 minutes. Add the sugar and garlic, and cook for another minute.

Deglaze and Simmer: Add the white wine to deglaze the pot, scraping up any browned bits from the bottom. Add the beef broth, bay leaf, thyme, salt, and pepper. Bring to a boil, then reduce heat and simmer for 30 minutes.

Prepare the Bread: Preheat the oven to 200°C (400°F). Arrange the baguette slices on a baking sheet and toast in the oven until golden brown.

Assemble and Serve: Ladle the soup into oven-safe bowls. Top each bowl with toasted baguette slices and a generous amount of grated Gruyère cheese. Place the bowls under a broiler until the cheese is melted and bubbly. Serve hot.

## 3.2 Escargots à la Bourguignonne

**ingredients**:

- 24 canned escargots, drained and rinsed
- 1/2 cup unsalted butter, softened
- 2 cloves garlic, minced
- 2 tablespoons finely chopped parsley
- 1 tablespoon finely chopped shallots
- 1 tablespoon dry white wine
- Salt and pepper to taste
- 24 small mushroom caps or escargot shells

*Instructions*:

Prepare the Butter: In a bowl, mix the softened butter with garlic, parsley, shallots, white wine, salt, and pepper until well combined.

Stuff the Escargots: Preheat the oven to 180°C (350°F). Place an escargot in each mushroom cap or shell. Top each with a small amount of the garlic butter mixture.

Bake: Arrange the stuffed escargots on a baking sheet and bake for about 10-12 minutes until the butter is bubbling and the escargots are heated through. Serve immediately.

## 3.3 Ratatouille

**ingredients**:

- 1 small eggplant, diced
- 1 zucchini, diced
- 1 yellow squash, diced
- 1 red bell pepper, diced
- 1 yellow bell pepper, diced
- 1 onion, chopped
- 3 cloves garlic, minced
- 4 tablespoons olive oil
- 1 can (400g) diced tomatoes
- 1 teaspoon dried herbes de Provence
- Salt and pepper to taste
- Fresh basil for garnish

*Instructions*:

Cook the Vegetables: In a large skillet, heat 2 tablespoons of olive oil over medium heat. Add the eggplant and cook until soft. Remove and set aside. Add the remaining olive oil to the skillet and cook the zucchini, squash, bell peppers, and onion until tender. Add the garlic and cook for another minute.

Combine and Simmer: Return the eggplant to the skillet. Add the diced tomatoes, herbes de Provence, salt, and pepper. Simmer for 20-25 minutes until all the vegetables are tender and the flavors are well combined.

Serve: Garnish with fresh basil and serve hot or at room temperature.

## 3.4 Salade Niçoise

**ingredients:**

- 200g small new potatoes, boiled and halved
- 200g green beans, blanched
- 2 tomatoes, cut into wedges

- 1 small red onion, thinly sliced

- 1 can (200g) tuna in olive oil, drained

- 4 hard-boiled eggs, halved

- 1/2 cup black olives

- 2 tablespoons capers

- 4 anchovy fillets (optional)

- Mixed greens

For the Dressing:

- 1/4 cup olive oil

- 2 tablespoons red wine vinegar

- 1 teaspoon Dijon mustard

- 1 clove garlic, minced

- Salt and pepper to taste

### Instructions:

Prepare the Dressing: In a small bowl, whisk together the olive oil, red wine vinegar, Dijon mustard, garlic, salt, and pepper.

Assemble the Salad: On a large platter, arrange the mixed greens. Top with potatoes, green beans, tomatoes, red onion, tuna, eggs, olives, capers, and anchovies (if using).

Dress and Serve: Drizzle the dressing over the salad and serve immediately.

# 3.5 Gougères

**ingredients**:

- 120ml water
- 120ml milk
- 100g unsalted butter
- 1/2 teaspoon salt
- 1 cup all-purpose flour
- 4 large eggs
- 1 cup grated Gruyère cheese
- 1/4 teaspoon ground nutmeg

**Instructions**:

Prepare the Dough: Preheat the oven to 200°C (400°F). In a saucepan, combine water, milk, butter, and salt. Bring to a boil. Add the flour all at once and stir vigorously until the mixture forms a ball and pulls away from the sides of the pan. Remove from heat and let cool slightly.

Add the Eggs and Cheese: Transfer the dough to a bowl. Add the eggs one at a time, beating well after each addition. Stir in the grated Gruyère cheese and nutmeg.

Shape and Bake: Drop tablespoon-sized mounds of dough onto a baking sheet lined with parchment paper. Bake for 20-25 minutes until puffed and golden brown. Serve warm.

# Chapter 4: Main Courses

## 4.1 Coq au Vin

**ingredients**:

- 1 whole chicken, cut into serving pieces
- Salt and pepper to taste
- 4 tablespoons olive oil
- 200g bacon, diced
- 1 large onion, chopped
- 2 carrots, sliced
- 3 cloves garlic, minced
- 2 tablespoons flour
- 1 bottle red wine (Burgundy or Pinot Noir)
- 2 cups chicken broth
- 1 bay leaf
- 1 teaspoon fresh thyme leaves
- 200g mushrooms, sliced
- Fresh parsley for garnish

**Instructions:**

Prepare the Chicken: Season the chicken pieces with salt and pepper. In a large Dutch oven, heat 2 tablespoons of olive oil over medium heat. Brown the chicken pieces on all sides, then remove and set aside.

Cook the Bacon and Vegetables: In the same pot, add the remaining olive oil and cook the bacon until crispy. Remove the bacon and set aside. Add the onion, carrots, and garlic to the pot and cook until the vegetables are softened.

Combine and Simmer: Sprinkle the flour over the vegetables and stir to coat. Gradually add the wine and chicken broth, stirring constantly. Add the bay leaf, thyme, browned chicken, and bacon back to the pot. Bring to a boil, then reduce heat and simmer for 45 minutes.

Add the Mushrooms: In a separate pan, sauté the mushrooms in a little olive oil until browned. Add the mushrooms to the pot and continue to simmer for another 15 minutes.

Serve: Garnish with fresh parsley and serve hot, accompanied by crusty bread or mashed potatoes.

## 4.2 Boeuf Bourguignon

### ingredients:

- 1.5kg beef chuck, cut into large cubes
- Salt and pepper to taste
- 3 tablespoons olive oil

- 200g bacon, diced
- 2 onions, chopped
- 3 carrots, sliced
- 3 cloves garlic, minced
- 2 tablespoons flour
- 1 bottle red wine (Burgundy or Pinot Noir)
- 2 cups beef broth
- 1 bay leaf
- 1 teaspoon fresh thyme leaves
- 200g mushrooms, sliced
- Fresh parsley for garnish

Instructions:

Prepare the Beef: Season the beef cubes with salt and pepper. In a large Dutch oven, heat 1 tablespoon of olive oil over medium-high heat. Brown the beef in batches, then remove and set aside.

Cook the Bacon and Vegetables: In the same pot, add the remaining olive oil and cook the bacon until crispy. Remove the bacon and set aside. Add the onions, carrots, and garlic to the pot and cook until the vegetables are softened.

Combine and Simmer: Sprinkle the flour over the vegetables and stir to coat. Gradually add the wine and beef broth, stirring constantly. Add the bay leaf, thyme, browned beef, and bacon back to the pot. Bring to a boil, then reduce heat and simmer for 1.5 to 2 hours until the beef is tender.

Add the Mushrooms: In a separate pan, sauté the mushrooms in a little olive oil until browned. Add the mushrooms to the pot and continue to simmer for another 15 minutes.

Serve: Garnish with fresh parsley and serve hot, accompanied by crusty bread or mashed potatoes.

## 4.3 Duck à l'Orange

**ingredients:**

- 1 whole duck (about 2kg)
- Salt and pepper to taste
- 1 orange, quartered
- 4 tablespoons honey
- 2 tablespoons red wine vinegar
- 1 cup chicken broth
- 1/2 cup orange juice
- Zest of 1 orange

- 1 tablespoon cornstarch mixed with 2 tablespoons water

***Instructions***:

Prepare the Duck: Preheat the oven to 180°C (350°F). Rinse the duck and pat dry. Season the cavity with salt and pepper and place the orange quarters inside. Truss the duck and place it on a rack in a roasting pan.

Roast the Duck: Roast the duck for about 1.5 to 2 hours until the skin is crisp and the meat is tender. Baste occasionally with the pan juices.

Prepare the Sauce: In a saucepan, combine the honey, red wine vinegar, chicken broth, orange juice, and orange zest. Bring to a boil, then reduce heat and simmer until reduced by half. Stir in the cornstarch mixture and cook until the sauce thickens.

**Serve**: *Carve the duck and serve with the orange sauce on the side.*

# 4.4 Ratatouille

**ingredients:**

- 1 small eggplant, diced
- 1 zucchini, diced

- 1 yellow squash, diced
- 1 red bell pepper, diced
- 1 yellow bell pepper, diced
- 1 onion, chopped
- 3 cloves garlic, minced
- 4 tablespoons olive oil
- 1 can (400g) diced tomatoes
- 1 teaspoon dried herbes de Provence
- Salt and pepper to taste
- Fresh basil for garnish

***Instructions:***

Cook the Vegetables: In a large skillet, heat 2 tablespoons of olive oil over medium heat. Add the eggplant and cook until soft. Remove and set aside. Add the remaining olive oil to the skillet and cook the zucchini, squash, bell peppers, and onion until tender. Add the garlic and cook for another minute.

Combine and Simmer: Return the eggplant to the skillet. Add the diced tomatoes, herbes de Provence, salt, and pepper. Simmer for 20-25 minutes until all the vegetables are tender and the flavors are well combined.

Serve: Garnish with fresh basil and serve hot or at room temperature.

# 4.5 Quiche Lorraine

ingredients:

- 1 pie crust (store-bought or homemade)
- 200g bacon, diced
- 1 small onion, finely chopped
- 3 large eggs
- 200ml heavy cream
- Salt and pepper to taste
- 100g Gruyère cheese, grated

*Instructions*:

Prepare the Crust: Preheat the oven to 180°C (350°F). Roll out the pie crust and fit it into a tart pan. Prick the bottom with a fork and pre-bake for 10 minutes.

Prepare the Filling: In a skillet, cook the bacon until crispy. Remove and drain on paper towels. In the same skillet, cook the onion until soft. In a bowl, whisk together the eggs, cream, salt, and pepper.

Assemble and Bake: Spread the bacon and onion over the pre-baked crust. Pour the egg mixture over the top and sprinkle with grated cheese. Bake for 25-30 minutes until the filling is set and the top is golden brown. Let cool slightly before slicing.

# Chapter 5: Desserts

## 5.1 Crème Brûlée

**ingredients**:

- 2 cups heavy cream
- 1 vanilla bean, split and scraped (or 1 teaspoon vanilla extract)
- 5 large egg yolks
- 1/2 cup granulated sugar
- 1/4 cup brown sugar (for caramelizing)

***Instructions:***

Prepare the Cream: Preheat the oven to 150°C (300°F). In a saucepan, combine the heavy cream and vanilla bean (or extract) and bring to a simmer over medium heat. Remove from heat and let it sit for a few minutes to infuse the vanilla flavor.

Beat the Yolks: In a bowl, whisk together the egg yolks and granulated sugar until pale and thick. Gradually whisk the warm cream into the egg mixture.

Bake: Pour the mixture into ramekins. Place the ramekins in a baking dish and add enough hot water to come halfway up the sides of the ramekins. Bake for 35-40 minutes until the custards are set but still slightly jiggly in the center. Remove from the water bath and let cool to room temperature. Refrigerate for at least 2 hours or overnight.

*Caramelize: Just before serving, sprinkle an even layer of brown sugar on top of each custard. Use a kitchen torch to caramelize the sugar until it forms a crispy, golden crust. Serve immediately.*

## 5.2 Tarte Tatin

**ingredients:**

- 6-8 apples (such as Granny Smith), peeled, cored, and quartered
- 1/2 cup unsalted butter
- 1 cup granulated sugar
- 1 sheet puff pastry, thawed

*Instructions:*

Prepare the Caramel: Preheat the oven to 190°C (375°F). In a heavy ovenproof skillet, melt the butter over medium heat. Add the sugar and cook, stirring constantly, until it turns a deep golden brown.

Add the Apples: Arrange the apple quarters in a circular pattern in the skillet, packing them tightly. Cook for about 15 minutes, occasionally spooning the caramel over the apples, until they are partially tender.

Top with Pastry: Roll out the puff pastry to fit over the skillet. Lay the pastry over the apples, tucking the edges down around the apples.

Bake: Place the skillet in the oven and bake for 25-30 minutes until the pastry is golden brown and puffed. Let the tart cool for a few minutes, then carefully invert it onto a serving plate. Serve warm.

## 5.3 Chocolate Soufflé

**ingredients**:

- 4 tablespoons unsalted butter, plus extra for greasing
- 2 tablespoons all-purpose flour
- 1 cup whole milk
- 200g dark chocolate, chopped
- 4 large egg yolks
- 5 large egg whites
- 1/4 cup granulated sugar
- Powdered sugar for dusting

*Instructions*:

Prepare the Ramekins: Preheat the oven to 190°C (375°F). Grease the inside of 6 ramekins with butter and dust with granulated sugar.

Make the Base: In a saucepan, melt the butter over medium heat. Add the flour and cook, stirring constantly, for 1-2 minutes. Gradually whisk in the milk and cook until the mixture thickens. Remove from heat and stir in the chopped chocolate until melted and smooth. Whisk in the egg yolks.

Beat the Egg Whites: In a clean bowl, beat the egg whites until soft peaks form. Gradually add the granulated sugar and continue to beat until stiff peaks form.

Combine and Bake: Gently fold the egg whites into the chocolate mixture in three additions. Divide the mixture among the prepared ramekins and place them on a baking sheet. Bake for 15-18 minutes until the soufflés are puffed and set. Dust with powdered sugar and serve immediately.

## 5.4 Madeleines

**ingredients**:

- 1/2 cup unsalted butter, melted and cooled
- 2/3 cup granulated sugar
- 3 large eggs

- 1 teaspoon vanilla extract
- 1 cup all-purpose flour
- 1/2 teaspoon baking powder
- 1/4 teaspoon salt
- Zest of 1 lemon
- Powdered sugar for dusting

*Instructions*:

Prepare the Batter: In a bowl, whisk together the sugar, eggs, and vanilla extract until pale and thick. Sift in the flour, baking powder, and salt, and gently fold into the egg mixture. Add the lemon zest and melted butter, folding gently until combined. Cover the batter and refrigerate for at least 30 minutes.

Bake: Preheat the oven to 190°C (375°F). Grease a madeleine pan with butter and dust with flour. Spoon the batter into the prepared pan, filling each mold about three-quarters full. Bake for 10-12 minutes until the edges are golden brown and the centers spring back when lightly touched.

Cool and Serve: Remove the madeleines from the pan and let cool on a wire rack. Dust with powdered sugar before serving.

# 5.5 Clafoutis

**ingredients**:

- 400g cherries, pitted
- 3 large eggs
- 1/2 cup granulated sugar
- 1 cup whole milk
- 1/2 cup heavy cream
- 1 teaspoon vanilla extract
- 1/2 cup all-purpose flour
- 1/4 teaspoon salt
- Powdered sugar for dusting

*Instructions*:

Prepare the Cherries: Preheat the oven to 180°C (350°F). Grease a baking dish with butter and arrange the pitted cherries evenly in the dish.

Make the Batter: In a blender, combine the eggs, sugar, milk, cream, vanilla extract, flour, and salt. Blend until smooth.

Bake: Pour the batter over the cherries. Bake for 35-40 minutes until the clafoutis is puffed and golden brown around the edges. Let cool slightly.

**Serve**: *Dust with powdered sugar and serve warm.*

# Chapter 6: Bistro Favorites

## 6.1 Steak Frites

**ingredients:**

- 2 ribeye or sirloin steaks (about 1 inch thick)
- Salt
- Freshly ground black pepper
- Olive oil
- For the Frites:
- 4 large russet potatoes
- Vegetable oil (for frying)
- Salt
- For Béarnaise Sauce:
- 60ml white wine vinegar
- 1 shallot, finely chopped
- 1 tablespoon fresh tarragon, chopped
- 3 egg yolks
- 200g clarified butter
- Salt
- Freshly ground black pepper

*Instructions:*

1. **Prepare the Steak:**

2. **Bring to Room Temperature**: Remove the steaks from the refrigerator and let them come to room temperature.

3. **season**: Rub the steaks with olive oil, then season generously with salt and freshly ground black pepper.

4. **Cook the Steak:**

5. **Preheat Skillet**: Heat a cast-iron skillet over high heat until smoking hot.

6. **Sear:** Add a small amount of oil to the skillet, then place the steaks in the skillet. Cook without moving for 3-4 minutes to develop a deep crust. Flip the steaks and cook for another 3-4 minutes for medium-rare, or until the desired doneness is reached.

7. **Rest:** Remove the steaks from the skillet and let them rest for 5-10 minutes.

8. **Prepare the Frites:**

9. **Cut Potatoes**: Peel the potatoes and cut them into thin strips. Rinse in cold water to remove excess starch and pat dry thoroughly.

10. **First Fry**: Heat vegetable oil in a large pot to 325°F (163°C). Fry the potatoes in batches for 5-6 minutes until tender but not browned. Remove and drain on paper towels.

11. **Second Fry**: Increase the oil temperature to 375°F (190°C). Fry the potatoes again in batches until golden brown and crispy, about 2-3 minutes. Drain on paper towels and season with salt immediately.

12. **Prepare Béarnaise Sauce:**

13. **Reduce**: In a small saucepan, combine white wine vinegar, shallot, and tarragon. Simmer until the liquid is nearly evaporated. Strain and let cool slightly.

14. **Emulsify**: In a heatproof bowl, whisk together egg yolks and the vinegar

reduction. Place the bowl over a pot of simmering water and slowly whisk in clarified butter until the sauce is thick and emulsified. Season with salt, pepper, and fresh tarragon.

*Serve:*

Plate: Place the rested steak on a plate, accompanied by a generous portion of crispy frites.Sauce: Drizzle Béarnaise sauce over the steak or serve it on the side for dipping.

Enjoy: Serve immediately, perhaps with a simple green salad and a light vinaigrette to balance the richness of the meal.


## 6.2 Croque Monsieur and Croque Madame
**ingredients:**

***For the Sandwiches:***

- 8 slices of white bread
- 4 slices of ham
- 4 slices of Gruyère or Emmental cheese
- 2 tablespoons Dijon mustard
- 2 tablespoons butter, softened
- 4 eggs (for Croque Madame)

***For the Béchamel Sauce:***

- 2 tablespoons butter
- 2 tablespoons all-purpose flour
- 1 cup milk
- Salt
- Freshly ground black pepper
- Pinch of nutmeg

***Instructions:***

Prepare the Béchamel Sauce:

**Melt Butter**: In a small saucepan over medium heat, melt the butter.

**Make Roux**: Add the flour and whisk continuously for about 1-2 minutes until it forms a smooth paste (roux).

**Add Milk**: Gradually add the milk, whisking constantly to prevent lumps. Continue to cook and whisk until the sauce thickens.

**season**: Season with salt, pepper, and a pinch of nutmeg. Remove from heat and set aside.

Assemble the Sandwiches:

**Preheat Oven:** Preheat your oven to 375°F (190°C).

**Prepare Bread:** Spread Dijon mustard on one side of each slice of bread.

**Layer Ingredients**: On 4 slices of bread, place a slice of ham and a slice of cheese. Top with the remaining slices of bread, mustard side down.

**Butter Bread**: Spread softened butter on the outside of each sandwich.

<u>Cook Sandwiches:</u>

toast: In a large skillet over medium heat, toast the sandwiches until golden brown on both sides, about 3-4 minutes per side.

Add Béchamel: Place the toasted sandwiches on a baking sheet. Spoon a generous amount of béchamel sauce over the top of each sandwich, then sprinkle with additional cheese.

Bake: Bake in the preheated oven for about 5-7 minutes, or until the cheese is melted and bubbly.

For Croque Monsieur:


Serve: Once the sandwiches are baked, remove from the oven and serve hot.

For Croque Madame:

**Cook Eggs:** While the sandwiches are baking, heat a small amount of butter in a non-stick skillet over medium heat. Fry the eggs sunny-side up or over-easy, depending on your preference.

Top with Egg: Place a fried egg on top of each sandwich after removing them from the oven.

Serve:


Serve the Croque Monsieur and Croque Madame hot, with a simple green salad on the side if desired.

Enjoy this classic French comfort food, perfect for a hearty breakfast, brunch, or lunch.

In this way, you can savor the rich, gooey goodness of Croque Monsieur and the added indulgence of Croque Madame, with its perfectly fried egg on top.

# 6.3 Moules Marinières

**ingredients:**

- 2 pounds (1 kg) fresh mussels
- 2 tablespoons butter
- 2 shallots, finely chopped
- 3 cloves garlic, minced
- 1 cup dry white wine
- 1 cup heavy cream
- 1 bay leaf
- 2 sprigs fresh thyme
- 1 small bunch fresh parsley, chopped
- Salt and freshly ground black pepper
- 1 lemon, cut into wedges (for serving)
- Crusty bread (for serving)

*Instructions:*

**Prepare the Mussels:**

Clean Mussels: Rinse the mussels under cold running water. Scrub the shells to remove any debris and pull out the beards (the fibrous threads sticking out from the shells). Discard any mussels that are open and do not close when tapped.

**Cook the Mussels:**

Sauté Aromatics: In a large pot or Dutch oven, melt the butter over medium heat. Add the chopped shallots and garlic, and sauté until they are soft and fragrant, about 3-4 minutes.

Add Wine and Herbs: Pour in the white wine and add the bay leaf and thyme sprigs. Increase the heat to high and bring the mixture to a boil.

Add Mussels: Add the cleaned mussels to the pot, cover with a lid, and cook for about 5-7 minutes, shaking the pot occasionally, until the mussels have opened. Discard any mussels that remain closed. Finish with Cream: Reduce the heat to medium and stir in the heavy cream. Cook for another 2-3 minutes until the sauce is well combined and heated through. Season with salt and freshly ground black pepper to taste.

Serve:

Plate: Using a slotted spoon, transfer the cooked mussels to serving bowls. Pour the sauce over the mussels, making sure to include the shallots and garlic.

Garnish: Sprinkle the chopped parsley over the top.

Accompaniments: Serve immediately with lemon wedges on the side and crusty bread to soak up the delicious sauce.

## 6.4 Poulet Rôti (Roast Chicken)

ingredients:

- 1 whole chicken (about 4-5 pounds)
- 2 tablespoons olive oil
- 4 cloves garlic, minced
- 1 lemon, halved
- 1 bunch fresh thyme
- 1 bunch fresh rosemary
- Salt

- Freshly ground black pepper

- 4 tablespoons butter, softened

- 1 onion, quartered

- 2 carrots, cut into large chunks

- 2 celery stalks, cut into large chunks

- 1 cup chicken broth

*Instructions:*

Prepare the Chicken:

**Preheat Oven**: Preheat your oven to 425°F (220°C).

Season Chicken: Rinse the chicken inside and out, then pat it dry with paper towels. Rub the chicken all over with olive oil, and season generously with salt and freshly ground black pepper.

**Stuff Chicken:** Stuff the cavity of the chicken with the minced garlic, lemon halves, thyme, and rosemary.

**Truss and Butter the Chicken:**

**Truss Chicken:** Tie the legs of the chicken together with kitchen twine, and tuck the wing tips under the body of the chicken to ensure even cooking.

**Butter Chicken**: Rub the softened butter evenly over the skin of the chicken.

Prepare the Vegetables:

**Arrange Vegetables**: Place the onion, carrots, and celery in a large roasting pan. Pour the chicken broth over the vegetables.

**Place Chicken:** Place the prepared chicken on top of the vegetables in the roasting pan.

<u>**Roast the Chicken:**</u>

Initial Roast: Roast the chicken in the preheated oven for about 15 minutes. This high heat helps to crisp the skin.

Lower Heat: Reduce the oven temperature to 375°F (190°C) and continue roasting for about 1 hour and 15 minutes, or until the internal temperature of the chicken reaches 165°F (74°C) when measured in the thickest part of the thigh.

Baste: Baste the chicken with the pan juices every 20 minutes to keep it moist and flavorful.

***Rest and Serve:***

Rest Chicken: Once the chicken is done, remove it from the oven and let it rest for about 15 minutes. This allows the juices to redistribute throughout the meat.

Carve: Carve the chicken and serve it with the roasted vegetables from the pan. Spoon some of the pan juices over the chicken and vegetables for extra flavor.

Accompaniments:

*Serve:* **Poulet Rôti is traditionally served with a simple green salad, crusty bread, or roasted potatoes. Enjoy this classic French roast chicken,** *full of rich and comforting flavors, perfect for a family dinner or a special occasion.*

## 6.5 Bouillabaisse

ingredients:

- **<u>For the Broth:</u>**
- 2 tablespoons olive oil
- 1 large onion, chopped
- 2 leeks, white parts only, chopped
- 4 cloves garlic, minced
- 1 fennel bulb, chopped
- 2 large tomatoes, chopped
- 1 teaspoon saffron threads
- 2 bay leaves
- 1 teaspoon dried thyme
- 1 teaspoon dried orange zest
- Salt
- Freshly ground black pepper
- 4 cups fish stock or water
- 1 cup dry white wine
- 2 tablespoons tomato paste

<u>**For the Seafood:**</u>

- 1 pound firm white fish (such as cod or sea bass), cut into chunks
- 1 pound mussels, cleaned and debearded
- 1 pound clams, cleaned
- 1 pound shrimp, peeled and deveined
- 1/2 pound squid, cleaned and cut into rings
- For the Rouille (optional):
- 1 slice of white bread, crust removed
- 1 roasted red pepper
- 2 cloves garlic
- 1 egg yolk
- 1 teaspoon Dijon mustard
- 1/2 cup olive oil
- Salt
- Freshly ground black pepper

*Instructions:*

<u>**Prepare the Broth**</u>:

Sauté Vegetables: In a large pot or Dutch oven, heat the olive oil over medium heat. Add the chopped onion, leeks, garlic, and fennel. Sauté until the vegetables are soft and fragrant, about 8-10 minutes.

Add Tomatoes and Herbs: Add the chopped tomatoes, saffron threads, bay leaves, dried thyme, and dried orange zest. Season with salt and freshly ground black pepper.

Add Liquids: Pour in the fish stock (or water) and white wine. Stir in the tomato paste. Bring the mixture to a boil, then reduce the heat and let it simmer for about 30 minutes to develop the flavors.

**Prepare the Seafood:**

Add Fish: Add the chunks of white fish to the simmering broth. Cook for about 5 minutes.

Add Shellfish: Add the mussels, clams, shrimp, and squid to the pot. Cover and cook for another 5-7 minutes, or until the mussels and clams have opened and the shrimp and squid are cooked through. Discard any shellfish that do not open.

Prepare the Rouille (optional):


Blend Ingredients: In a food processor, blend the white bread, roasted red pepper, garlic, egg yolk, and Dijon mustard until smooth.

Add Oil: With the processor running, slowly drizzle in the olive oil until the mixture is thick and emulsified. Season with salt and freshly ground black pepper to taste.

# Chapter 7: Drinks

## 7.1 Kir Royale

**ingredients**:

- 1/2 ounce crème de cassis
- 4 ounces Champagne or sparkling wine

*Instructions*:

Prepare the Glass: Chill a Champagne flute.

Mix: Add the crème de cassis to the flute.

top: Slowly pour in the Champagne or sparkling wine to fill the glass.

**Serve**: *Serve immediately.*

## 7.2 French 75

**ingredients**:

- 2 ounces gin
- 1 ounce fresh lemon juice
- 1/2 ounce simple syrup
- 4 ounces Champagne or sparkling wine
- Lemon twist for garnish

*Instructions*:

Mix: *In a shaker, combine the gin, lemon juice, and simple syrup. Fill with ice and shake well.*

*Strain: Strain into a chilled Champagne flute.*

top: Top with Champagne or sparkling wine.

Garnish: Garnish with a lemon twist and serve.

## 7.3 Café au Lait

**ingredients**:

- 1/2 cup freshly brewed strong coffee
- 1/2 cup steamed milk

*Instructions*:

Brew: Brew a strong coffee.

Steam: Steam the milk until it is hot and frothy.

Combine: Pour the coffee into a cup and add the steamed milk. Serve immediately.

## 7.4 Vin Chaud

**ingredients**:

- 1 bottle red wine
- 1/4 cup brandy
- 1/2 cup water
- 1/2 cup sugar
- 1 orange, sliced
- 1 lemon, sliced
- 4 cloves
- 2 cinnamon sticks

- 2 star anise

*Instructions*:

1. **Combine**: In a large pot, combine the wine, brandy, water, sugar, orange slices, lemon slices, cloves, cinnamon sticks, and star anise.
2. **heat:** Heat over medium-low heat until the mixture is hot but not boiling. Stir occasionally until the sugar is dissolved.
3. **Simmer**: Reduce heat to low and let it simmer for about 20 minutes.
4. **Strain and Serve:** Strain out the spices and fruit slices. Serve warm in mugs.

# 7.5 Pastis

**ingredients**:

- 1 ounce pastis (anise-flavored liqueur)
- 5 ounces cold water
- Ice cubes

*Instructions*:

1. **Prepare**: Fill a glass with ice cubes.
2. **Mix**: Pour the pastis over the ice.

3. **Dilute**: Add the cold water and stir gently. Serve immediately.

## 7.6 Sidecar

**ingredients:**

2 oz cognac

1 oz Cointreau (or triple sec)

3/4 oz fresh lemon juice

Lemon twist or orange twist (for garnish)

Sugar (for rimming the glass, optional)

**Instructions:**

Prepare Glass: If desired, rim the edge of a cocktail glass with sugar.

Shake Ingredients: In a cocktail shaker filled with ice, combine the cognac, Cointreau, and fresh lemon juice. Shake well.

Strain: Strain the mixture into the prepared glass.

Garnish: Garnish with a lemon or orange twist.

## 7.7 French Martini

**ingredients:**

2 oz vodka

1/2 oz Chambord (raspberry liqueur)

1 oz pineapple juice

Raspberry or lemon twist (for garnish)

**Instructions:**

Shake Ingredients: In a cocktail shaker filled with ice, combine the vodka, Chambord, and pineapple juice. Shake well.

Strain: Strain the mixture into a chilled martini glass.

Garnish: Garnish with a raspberry or a lemon twist.

## 7.8 Mimosa

**ingredients:**

2 oz orange juice (freshly squeezed, if possible)

4 oz Champagne or sparkling wine

Orange slice or twist (for garnish)

*Instructions:*

Pour Orange Juice: Pour the orange juice into a champagne flute.

Add Champagne: Slowly add the Champagne or sparkling wine.

Garnish: Garnish with an orange slice or twist.

# Chapter 8: Special Occasions

## 8.1 Beef Wellington

**ingredients:**

- 2 pounds beef tenderloin, trimmed
- Salt and pepper to taste
- 2 tablespoons olive oil
- 1/2 pound mushrooms, finely chopped
- 2 tablespoons unsalted butter
- 2 shallots, finely chopped
- 1/4 cup dry white wine
- 8 slices prosciutto
- 1 sheet puff pastry, thawed
- 1 egg, beaten

**Instructions:**

1. **Prepare the Beef:** Season the tenderloin with salt and pepper. Heat the olive oil in a large skillet over high heat. Sear the beef on all sides until browned, about 2-3 minutes per side. Remove from the skillet and let cool.

2. **Make the Duxelles**: In the same skillet, melt the butter over medium heat. Add the shallots and cook until soft. Add the mushrooms and cook until all the moisture has evaporated. Stir in the white wine and cook until absorbed. Remove from heat and let cool.

3. **Wrap the Beef**: Lay out the prosciutto slices on a piece of plastic wrap, slightly overlapping. Spread the duxelles over the prosciutto. Place the beef on top and roll it up tightly in the prosciutto, using the plastic wrap to help. Chill in the refrigerator for 30 minutes.

4. **Wrap in Pastry**: Preheat the oven to 200°C (400°F). Roll out the puff pastry on a lightly floured surface. Remove the plastic wrap from the beef and place it in the center of the pastry. Fold the pastry over the beef, sealing the edges. Brush with the beaten egg.

5. **Bake**: Place the wrapped beef on a baking sheet and bake for 25-30 minutes, until the pastry is golden brown and a meat thermometer

inserted into the center reads 125°F (51°C) for medium-rare. Let rest for 10 minutes before slicing and serving.

## 8.2 Coq au Vin

**ingredients**:

- 1 whole chicken, cut into 8 pieces
- Salt and pepper to taste
- 2 tablespoons olive oil
- 4 slices bacon, chopped
- 1 onion, chopped
- 2 carrots, chopped
- 2 garlic cloves, minced
- 2 tablespoons all-purpose flour
- 2 cups red wine
- 1 cup chicken broth
- 1 tablespoon tomato paste
- 1 bay leaf
- 4 sprigs thyme
- 1/2 pound mushrooms, quartered
- 1/2 cup pearl onions, peeled

*Instructions*:

1. **Prepare the Chicken**: Season the chicken pieces with salt and pepper. Heat the olive oil in a large Dutch oven

over medium-high heat. Brown the chicken on all sides, then remove and set aside.

2. **Cook the Bacon and Vegetables**: Add the bacon to the pot and cook until crispy. Remove with a slotted spoon and set aside. Add the onion, carrots, and garlic to the pot and cook until softened.

3. **Add Flour and Liquids**: Sprinkle the flour over the vegetables and stir to coat. Gradually add the wine and chicken broth, stirring constantly until the mixture thickens. Stir in the tomato paste, bay leaf, and thyme.

4. **Simmer**: Return the chicken and bacon to the pot. Add the mushrooms and pearl onions. Cover and simmer over low heat for about 45 minutes, until the chicken is tender and cooked through.

5. **Serve**: Remove the bay leaf and thyme sprigs. Serve the coq au vin hot with crusty bread or mashed potatoes.

# 8.3 Bouillabaisse

**ingredients**:

- 2 tablespoons olive oil
- 1 onion, chopped
- 1 leek, chopped
- 2 garlic cloves, minced
- 1 fennel bulb, chopped
- 1 large tomato, chopped
- 1/2 teaspoon saffron threads
- 1 teaspoon dried thyme
- 1 bay leaf
- 1/2 cup dry white wine
- 4 cups fish stock
- 1/2 pound firm white fish (such as cod), cut into chunks
- 1/2 pound shellfish (such as mussels or clams), scrubbed
- 1/2 pound shrimp, peeled and deveined
- 1/2 pound squid, cleaned and cut into rings
- Salt and pepper to taste
- 1/4 cup chopped fresh parsley
- Crusty bread for serving

***Instructions***:

1. **Prepare the Base**: Heat the olive oil in a large pot over medium heat. Add the onion, leek, garlic, and fennel. Cook

until softened. Add the tomato, saffron, thyme, and bay leaf. Cook for a few more minutes.

2. **Add Liquids**: Pour in the white wine and fish stock. Bring to a boil, then reduce heat and simmer for 20 minutes.

3. **Add Seafood**: Add the fish, shellfish, shrimp, and squid to the pot. Simmer gently until the seafood is cooked through, about 5-7 minutes. Season with salt and pepper.

4. **Serve**: Remove the bay leaf. Sprinkle with fresh parsley and serve hot with crusty bread.

# 8.4 Galette des Rois

**ingredients**:

- 2 sheets puff pastry
- 1/2 cup almond flour
- 1/2 cup granulated sugar
- 1/4 cup unsalted butter, softened
- 2 large eggs
- 1 teaspoon almond extract
- 1 egg yolk (for egg wash)
- Powdered sugar for dusting

- 1 fève (a small trinket) or whole almond (optional)

**Instructions**:

1. **Prepare the Filling**: In a bowl, mix the almond flour, granulated sugar, butter, eggs, and almond extract until smooth.

2. **Assemble the Galette**: Preheat the oven to 190°C (375°F). Roll out one sheet of puff pastry on a baking sheet. Spread the almond filling evenly over the pastry, leaving a 1-inch border. If using a fève, place it in the filling.

3. **Top with Pastry**: Lay the second sheet of puff pastry over the filling. Press the edges to seal. Use a knife to score a decorative pattern on the top and brush with the egg yolk.

4. **Bake**: Bake for 20-25 minutes until the pastry is golden brown and puffed. Let cool slightly.

5. **Serve**: *Dust with powdered sugar before serving. Traditionally, the person who finds the fève in their slice becomes the "king" or "queen" for the day.*

# 8.5 Bûche de Noël

**ingredients**:

- 4 large eggs
- 1/2 cup granulated sugar
- 1/2 cup all-purpose flour
- 1/4 cup cocoa powder
- 1 teaspoon baking powder
- 1/4 teaspoon salt
- 1 teaspoon vanilla extract
- 1/2 cup heavy cream
- 1/2 cup powdered sugar
- 1/4 cup unsalted butter, softened
- 1/2 teaspoon vanilla extract
- 1/2 cup dark chocolate, melted
- Powdered sugar for dusting
- Fresh berries and mint leaves for garnish

*Instructions*:

1. **Prepare the Cake**: Preheat the oven to 180°C (350°F). Line a baking sheet with parchment paper. In a bowl, beat the eggs and granulated sugar until thick and pale. Sift together the flour, cocoa

powder, baking powder, and salt, then fold into the egg mixture. Stir in the vanilla extract. Spread the batter evenly on the baking sheet and bake for 10-12 minutes.

2. **Roll the Cake**: While the cake is still warm, roll it up in a clean kitchen towel dusted with powdered sugar. Let cool completely.

3. **Make the Filling**: In a bowl, whip the heavy cream and powdered sugar until stiff peaks form. Carefully unroll the cake and spread the whipped cream over the surface. Roll the cake back up without the towel.

4. **Make the Frosting**: In a bowl, beat the butter until creamy. Add the melted chocolate and vanilla extract, and beat until smooth. Frost the outside of the cake with the chocolate mixture, using a fork to create a bark-like texture.

5. **Serve**: Dust with powdered sugar and garnish with fresh berries and mint leaves. Slice and serve.

# Chapter 9: Seasonal and Special Occasions

The rhythm of French life is deeply intertwined with the changing seasons and the calendar's array of holidays and celebrations. Each season brings its own bounty of fresh ingredients, flavors, and traditions, and French cuisine makes the most of these. From the vibrant farmers' markets of spring to the hearty, comforting dishes of winter, there's always something to celebrate. This chapter will guide you through the culinary delights of each season and offer inspiration for holiday feasts, ensuring your table is always brimming with the best of what France has to offer.

## 9.1 Holiday Feasts

French holiday feasts are a time-honored tradition, where family and friends gather to share indulgent meals that showcase the country's rich culinary heritage. Christmas, New Year's Eve, and Easter each have their own unique dishes and customs.

Christmas is perhaps the most magical time of year in France, with cities and villages alike adorned with twinkling lights and festive decorations. The centerpiece of the Christmas meal is often a roast bird, such as a turkey or capon, stuffed with chestnuts and served with a rich, savory gravy. Foie gras, oysters, and smoked salmon are popular starters, while for dessert, no Christmas table is complete without a Bûche de Noël, a decadent yule log cake made of sponge cake and buttercream, often decorated to look like a real log.

New Year's Eve, known as "La Saint-Sylvestre," is celebrated with a grand feast called "Le Réveillon de la Saint-Sylvestre." This meal is typically more luxurious than the Christmas dinner and may include dishes like lobster, caviar, and truffles. Champagne flows freely, and the evening is capped off with a galette des rois, a flaky pastry filled with almond cream, to celebrate Epiphany.

Easter is another significant holiday, marked by the arrival of spring and a feast that often features lamb as the main course. A succulent leg of lamb roasted with garlic and rosemary is a classic choice, accompanied by fresh spring vegetables such as asparagus, peas, and new potatoes. Desserts might include chocolate eggs and a gâteau de Pâques, a light, airy cake often decorated with spring flowers.

## 9.2 Springtime in Paris

Spring in Paris is a time of renewal and awakening, as the city sheds its winter coat and bursts into bloom. The markets are overflowing with fresh produce, and the longer days and warmer weather make it the perfect time for leisurely meals enjoyed al fresco. One of the highlights of springtime in Paris is the arrival of asparagus, which is celebrated with dishes that showcase its delicate flavor. A simple asparagus salad with a lemon vinaigrette, or asparagus wrapped in prosciutto and roasted, are both delicious ways to enjoy this seasonal treat. Other spring vegetables, like peas and fava beans, are also at their peak and can be found in dishes like a vibrant spring vegetable risotto or a light, brothy vegetable soup.

Easter is a time for celebration, and no Easter table is complete without a lamb dish. A leg of lamb, roasted with garlic and rosemary, is a classic choice, but a more modern take might include lamb chops with a mint and pea purée. Fresh herbs, like mint, tarragon, and chervil, are abundant in the spring and add a bright, fresh flavor to dishes.

Spring is also the season for strawberries, which are celebrated in desserts like tarte aux fraises, a simple yet elegant tart made with a buttery pastry crust, a creamy custard filling, and topped with fresh strawberries. Another favorite is fraisier, a layered cake filled with strawberries and cream, perfect for a springtime celebration.

## 9.3 Summer Picnics

Summer in France is a time for relaxation and enjoying the outdoors, and there's no better way to do that than with a picnic. Whether you're in a city park, by the seaside, or in the countryside, a French picnic is a leisurely affair, with an emphasis on fresh, simple ingredients and plenty of good wine.

A typical French picnic might include a selection of charcuterie, such as saucisson sec, pâté, and rillettes, along with a variety of cheeses like Brie, Camembert, and Roquefort. Fresh baguettes are a must, as are olives, pickles, and perhaps a jar of cornichons. For something heartier, a quiche or a savory tart, like a pissaladière from Provence, makes a great addition. Salads are also a staple of the French picnic. A classic niçoise salad, with tuna, hard-boiled eggs, green beans, and olives, is a perfect choice for a summer meal, as is a simple tomato and mozzarella salad, drizzled with olive oil and balsamic vinegar. For dessert, fresh fruit is always a good option, but a clafoutis, a baked custard with cherries, is a delightful way to end the meal.

Drinks are an important part of any French picnic, and a chilled rosé or a light, crisp white wine are perfect for a summer day. For something non-alcoholic, a citron pressé, which is essentially a DIY lemonade made with fresh lemons, sugar, and water, is refreshing and easy to make.

## 9.4 Autumn Harvest

Autumn in France is a time of abundance, as the summer's bounty gives way to the rich, earthy flavors of fall. The markets are filled with pumpkins, squash, apples, and pears, and it's a time for hearty, comforting dishes that warm the soul.

One of the highlights of the autumn harvest is the arrival of wild mushrooms, which are celebrated in dishes like a creamy mushroom soup or a rustic mushroom tart. Chestnuts are also in season and can be found in dishes like a chestnut and bacon stuffing, perfect for a roast chicken or turkey.

Game meats, like venison and pheasant, are also popular in the fall and can be found in dishes like a venison stew with red wine and juniper berries, or a roast pheasant with apples and sage. These dishes are often accompanied by root vegetables, like carrots, parsnips, and potatoes, which are roasted to perfection. Apples and pears are at their best in the fall and are used in a variety of desserts, from a simple apple tart to a more elaborate tarte Tatin, a caramelized upside-down apple tart. Pears are often poached in red wine and served with a dollop of crème fraîche for a simple yet elegant dessert.

# 9.5 Winter Comforts

Winter in France is a time for comfort and indulgence, as the cold weather calls for hearty, warming dishes that nourish the body and soul. It's a time for rich stews, creamy gratins, and decadent desserts.

One of the most iconic winter dishes in France is coq au vin, a slow-cooked chicken stew made with red wine, mushrooms, and bacon. Served with creamy mashed potatoes or crusty bread, it's the perfect dish for a cold winter's night. Another classic is boeuf bourguignon, a beef stew made with red wine, onions, and mushrooms, which is also slow-cooked to tender perfection.

Gratins are a staple of French winter cooking, with dishes like gratin dauphinois, made with thinly sliced potatoes, cream, and cheese, being particularly popular. Another favorite is a leek and ham gratin, which combines tender leeks with a creamy béchamel sauce and smoky ham.

Desserts in winter are rich and indulgent, with chocolate playing a starring role. A classic chocolate mousse, made with dark chocolate, eggs, and cream, is a simple yet luxurious treat. For something a bit more elaborate, a chocolate fondant, with a molten center, is sure to impress. And of course, no French winter would be complete without a galette des rois, a flaky pastry filled with almond cream, traditionally enjoyed in January to celebrate Epiphany.

Throughout the year, French cuisine offers a wealth of seasonal and holiday dishes that celebrate the best of what each season has to offer. Whether you're preparing a festive holiday feast or simply enjoying a leisurely summer picnic, these recipes will help you bring a taste of France to your table, no matter the occasion.

# Chapter 10: The Parisian Dining Experience

Paris, the city of lights, is also the city of gastronomic delights. The Parisian dining experience is unparalleled, offering a blend of tradition, innovation, and an unwavering commitment to quality. From the way a table is set to the etiquette observed during meals, every aspect of dining in Paris is infused with a rich cultural heritage. This chapter delves into the intricacies of the Parisian dining experience, providing practical advice on setting the table, mastering dining etiquette, hosting a quintessential French dinner party, understanding the importance of fresh ingredients, and exploring the city through its vibrant café culture.

## 10.1 Setting the Table

The art of setting a table in Paris is a reflection of the elegance and sophistication that defines the city's culinary scene. A well-set table is not just about aesthetics; it is about creating an ambiance that enhances the dining experience. Begin with a pristine white tablecloth, which serves as a blank canvas for the meal. The next step is to place the dinner plates at each setting, ensuring they are perfectly centered and evenly spaced.

Cutlery is arranged in the order of use, starting from the outside and working inwards. On the left of the plate, place the fork, and on the right, the knife with the blade facing the plate. The spoon, if needed, is placed to the right of the knife. Above the plate, arrange the dessert fork and spoon horizontally, with the fork pointing right and the spoon pointing left. Glasses are placed above the knives, with the water glass directly above the knife and the wine glasses arranged to the right.

Napkins are folded neatly and placed either on the plate or to the left of the forks. Finally, add a touch of Parisian charm with small details like a sprig of fresh herbs, a single flower in a vase, or elegant place cards. These elements come together to create a table that is both inviting and reflective of the culinary journey that awaits.

## 10.2 Dining Etiquette

Dining etiquette is an essential aspect of social interaction that often reflects one's upbringing, manners, and respect for others. The nuances of dining etiquette can vary greatly across cultures, but there are fundamental principles that are universally respected. Understanding and practicing proper dining etiquette can enhance your social experiences, whether you are attending a formal dinner, a casual meal with friends, or a business lunch. At the heart of dining etiquette is the concept of respect—respect for your fellow diners, for the host, and for the culinary art presented before you. One of the primary elements of dining etiquette is punctuality. Arriving on time for a meal is a sign of respect for the host's efforts and the time of other guests. If you anticipate being late, it is courteous to inform the host as soon as possible.

Once at the table, it's important to be mindful of your posture. Sitting up straight and keeping your elbows off the table are fundamental rules that convey attentiveness and respect. Slouching or sprawling can be perceived as laziness or disinterest. When you sit down, place your napkin on your lap. This simple act signifies that you are ready to begin the meal and understand the basics of dining etiquette.

The use of utensils can be a source of anxiety for many, especially in formal settings where there might be an array of forks, knives, and spoons. A good rule of thumb is to start from the outside and work your way in with each course. For example, the outermost fork is typically used for the appetizer, while the inner fork is for the main course. If you are ever in doubt, quietly observe your host or the most experienced diners at the table.

When it comes to eating your food, take small, manageable bites, and chew with your mouth closed. Speaking with your mouth full is considered rude and can be unpleasant for others to witness. Additionally, avoid making loud noises while chewing or drinking. It's these small actions that collectively contribute to the overall dining experience.

Engaging in conversation during a meal is encouraged, but the topics should be chosen with care. Controversial subjects such as politics, religion, or personal grievances are best avoided to maintain a pleasant atmosphere. Instead, opt for neutral topics such as travel, books, movies, or shared experiences that can include everyone in the conversation. Listening is just as important as speaking; showing genuine interest in others' contributions can foster a harmonious dining environment.

Passing food at the table should be done with consideration. Always pass dishes to the right, and if someone asks for a specific item, pass it directly to them rather than passing it around the entire table. When serving yourself, take moderate portions to ensure there is enough for everyone. If you need to reach for something that is not immediately accessible, it is polite to ask for it to be passed rather than stretching across the table.

Handling glassware correctly is another aspect of dining etiquette that can sometimes be overlooked. Wine glasses are typically held by the stem to avoid warming the wine with your hand. This also prevents fingerprints on the bowl of the glass, keeping it clean and presentable. When toasting, make eye contact with your fellow diners, and if you clink glasses, do so gently to avoid breakage.

In many cultures, it is customary to wait until everyone has been served before beginning to eat. This shows respect for the host and allows everyone to start the meal together. If you are the host, it is your responsibility to ensure that all guests are comfortable and have what they need. This may involve discreetly checking in with guests throughout the meal to see if they require anything.

If you need to leave the table during the meal, place your napkin on your chair to indicate that you will return. When you are finished eating, place your utensils parallel on your plate, with the handles resting on the rim. This signals to the server that you are done. Placing your napkin loosely folded to the left of your plate also indicates that you have finished your meal.

Gratitude is an integral part of dining etiquette. If you are a guest, always thank your host before leaving, expressing your appreciation for their hospitality and the meal. A handwritten thank-you note the following day is a gracious gesture that is often remembered and appreciated. If dining out, it is polite to thank the restaurant staff, particularly your server, for their service.

In business settings, dining etiquette can play a crucial role in making a good impression. Business meals often serve as informal interviews or opportunities to build relationships. In such scenarios, it is important to remain professional yet personable. Arriving on time, dressing appropriately, and following the lead of the host can make a significant impact. Avoid discussing sensitive business topics until after the meal unless the host initiates the conversation.

Cultural differences in dining etiquette are also important to consider, especially when traveling or dining with individuals from different backgrounds. What is considered polite in one culture might be seen as rude in another. For example, in some Asian cultures, it is customary to leave a small amount of food on your plate to show that you are satisfied, while in many Western cultures, finishing your plate is a sign of appreciation. Learning about and respecting these differences can prevent misunderstandings and demonstrate cultural sensitivity.

Children and dining etiquette is another area worth mentioning. Teaching children proper dining manners from a young age sets a foundation for respectful behavior in social settings. Encourage them to sit still, use their utensils correctly, and engage politely in conversation. Patience and gentle reminders can go a long way in helping children understand the importance of dining etiquette.

Lastly, technology has introduced new challenges to dining etiquette. The presence of smartphones at the table can be a distraction and is often considered disrespectful. Unless it is an emergency, it is best to keep your phone on silent and out of sight. Giving your full attention to the people you are dining with shows respect and fosters meaningful interactions.

## 10.3 Hosting a French Dinner Party

There is an undeniable charm to hosting a French dinner party, an event that seamlessly blends culinary delight with the art of conversation. Embarking on this journey requires careful planning, a dash of creativity, and an appreciation for the nuances that define French hospitality. The goal is to create an atmosphere where your guests feel both pampered and at ease, all while indulging in the rich flavors of French cuisine.

Preparation is key. Start by selecting a suitable date and sending out invitations well in advance. This allows your guests to clear their schedules and look forward to the event. While digital invitations are convenient, handwritten ones add a personal touch that can set the tone for the evening. Ensure your invitations include all necessary details, such as the date, time, dress code, and any special instructions.

Next, consider your guest list carefully. A French dinner party thrives on lively conversation, so aim for a mix of personalities who can engage with each other. Too many guests can make the event feel crowded, while too few might dampen the atmosphere. A group of six to eight is often ideal, allowing for intimate yet dynamic interactions.

The heart of any French dinner party is, of course, the menu. French cuisine is renowned for its diversity and sophistication, so selecting the right dishes is crucial. Begin with a light appetizer, such as gougères (cheese puffs) or a simple salad with vinaigrette. These small bites awaken the palate without overwhelming it.

For the main course, consider classic dishes like coq au vin or boeuf bourguignon. These hearty, slow-cooked meals are rich in flavor and can be prepared in advance, allowing you to spend more time with your guests. Accompany the main dish with seasonal vegetables and a fresh baguette. French cuisine places a strong emphasis on using fresh, high-quality ingredients, so visit your local market for the best produce.

Dessert is an opportunity to end the meal on a high note. Opt for something quintessentially French, such as tarte Tatin or crème brûlée. These desserts are elegant yet comforting, providing a satisfying conclusion to the dinner. Pair the dessert with a good coffee or a digestif like cognac to round off the meal.

Wine selection is another critical aspect. A well-chosen wine can elevate each course, enhancing the flavors and adding to the overall experience. Start with a light, crisp white wine for the appetizer, such as a Sauvignon Blanc or a Chablis. For the main course, a robust red like a Bordeaux or a Burgundy complements the rich flavors of the dish. Finish with a sweet wine or champagne for dessert. If you are unsure about wine pairings, consult a knowledgeable wine merchant who can offer recommendations based on your menu.

Setting the table is an art in itself. Use a crisp, white tablecloth as your base, and add cloth napkins for a touch of elegance. Arrange the cutlery according to the courses, starting from the outside and working inwards. Place wine glasses and water glasses appropriately, and consider using a centerpiece that reflects the season, such as fresh flowers or candles. The goal is to create a table that is both inviting and functional, allowing for easy conversation and serving.

As guests arrive, greet them warmly and offer a welcome drink. This could be a classic French aperitif like Kir Royale or a simple glass of champagne. Use this time to introduce guests to one another if they are not already acquainted, setting the stage for engaging interactions throughout the evening.

The flow of the evening is important to consider. Begin with the appetizer, allowing guests to mingle and settle in. Serve the main course once everyone is comfortable, and pace the meal to ensure that no one feels rushed. Engage in light conversation, steering clear of controversial topics. Instead, focus on subjects that are inclusive and interesting to all your guests.

Between courses, take the opportunity to share a bit about the dishes you have prepared. This not only adds a personal touch but also provides a natural pause in the conversation, allowing guests to savor each course. French dining is as much about the experience as it is about the food, so encourage your guests to enjoy the moment.

Music can enhance the ambiance of your dinner party. Choose a playlist that complements the mood—something light and unobtrusive. French jazz or classical music can provide a pleasant backdrop without overpowering the conversation.

As the evening draws to a close, offer your guests a digestif. This could be a fine brandy or a liqueur like Grand Marnier. It is a traditional way to end a French meal, aiding digestion and providing a final moment of relaxation before guests depart.

Thank your guests sincerely as they leave, expressing your appreciation for their company. A small token, such as a wrapped macaron or a sachet of lavender, can serve as a lovely parting gift and a reminder of the evening.

Reflecting on the success of your Frenchdinner party, you will likely find that the true essence lies not just in the food and wine, but in the connections fostered around the table. Hosting such an event is an act of love and care, a celebration of life's simple yet profound pleasures.

## 10.4 Exploring Paris Through Its Cafés

Parisian cafés are more than just places to grab a quick coffee; they are integral to the city's social and cultural fabric. Each café has its own unique charm and character, offering a glimpse into the daily life of Parisians.

Cafés are ubiquitous in Paris, lining the streets and filling the squares. They serve as meeting points, workspaces, and havens for relaxation. The tradition of café culture dates back to the 17th century, and today, it remains a cherished part of Parisian life.

One of the most iconic aspects of Parisian café culture is the art of people-watching. Parisians take their time at cafés, savoring their drinks and observing the world around them. Whether you're sitting at a sidewalk table on the Boulevard Saint-Germain or tucked away in a quiet corner of the Marais, there's always a fascinating scene unfolding.

Coffee is, of course, a staple of the café experience. The French typically enjoy a strong espresso, known simply as "un café." For a longer, milder coffee, order a "café allongé," similar to an Americano. In the morning, you might opt for a "café crème," which is similar to a latte and pairs perfectly with a buttery croissant.

Cafés also offer a variety of light meals and snacks. A classic choice is the croque-monsieur, a toasted ham and cheese sandwich that is both satisfying and delicious. For something more substantial, many cafés serve dishes like quiche Lorraine, salads, and charcuterie boards.

Exploring Paris through its cafés is a delightful way to experience the city's culinary diversity. Each arrondissement has its own standout spots, from the historic Café de Flore in Saint-Germain-des-Prés to the trendy Café Oberkampf in the 11th arrondissement. Take the time to visit different neighborhoods and discover the unique ambiance and specialties of each café.

In conclusion, the Parisian dining experience is a rich tapestry of traditions, flavors, and cultural nuances. By understanding the importance of setting the table, mastering dining etiquette, hosting a French dinner party, prioritizing fresh ingredients, and exploring the city's vibrant café culture, you can immerse yourself in the culinary heart of Paris. Whether you're a seasoned gourmet or an enthusiastic beginner, these insights will help you appreciate and recreate the magic of Parisian dining in your own home.

**Conclusion**

*Congratulations on completing your culinary journey through this cookbook! From delightful appetizers to decadent desserts, you now have a collection of recipes that will impress your friends and family. Remember, cooking is as much about creativity and joy as it is about following recipes. Feel free to experiment with different ingredients and make these dishes your own.*

**Bon appétit!**